© Copyright 2023- All rights rese

The content contained within this
transmitted without direct writte

Under no circumstances will any blame or legal responsibility be held against the publisher, or author, for any damages, reparation, or monetary loss due to the information contained within this book. Either directly or indirectly. You are responsible for your own choices, actions, and results.

Legal Notice:

This book is copyright protected. This book is only for personal use. You cannot amend, distribute, sell, use, quote or paraphrase any part, or the content within this book, without the consent of the author or publisher.

Disclaimer Notice:

Please note the information contained within this document is for educational and entertainment purposes only. All effort has been executed to present accurate, up to date, and reliable, complete information. No warranties of any kind are declared or implied. Readers acknowledge that the author is not engaging in the rendering of legal, financial, medical or professional advice. The content within this book has been derived from various sources. Please consult a licensed professional before attempting any techniques outlined in this book.

By reading this document, the reader agrees that under no circumstances is the author responsible for any losses, direct or indirect, which are incurred as a result of the use of the information contained within this document, including, but not limited to, — errors, omissions, or inaccuracies.

THANK YOU

As an avoidant myself, I know how challenging it can be to take the first step. You could have picked from dozens of other workbooks, yet you took a chance on this one. Thank you so much for supporting new authors.

As a sign of appreciation, you can find a freebie at the end of the book. I hope this workbook will support you in your journey!

Alex Kingsman

Freebie
Freebie
Freebie
Freebie

Page 89

TABLE OF CONTENT

1	Prologue
2	Are you really afraid of commitment?
3	List of commitments
5	Are you really afraid of losing your independence?
6	Dismissive avoidant workbook benefits
7	What is attachment?
8	Attachment types
13	Children vs adults
15	Quiz
23	Why does avoidant attachment exist?
24	What are the advantages of being avoidant?
26	What is the next step?
26	What you might get wrong about healing avoidant attachment
27	How can you stop forecasting a future full of loneliness and pain?

TABLE OF CONTENT

28	Search for glimmers
32	What type of burden are you carrying?
35	Parentification
38	Enmeshment
43	What are you really feeling?
45	The Burning Stove
47	Why do emotions confuse us?
48	How to safely experience emotions
49	R.A.I.N.
54	Why should you try?
57	Emotional supression
59	The real work
59	Emotional vocabulary
62	Why should you identify the location of emotion in your body?

TABLE OF CONTENT

64	Are you really putting yourself first?
65	Owning your own wishes
67	Sabotaging intimacy
72	Humanizing your current relationship (or potential relationship)
73	Idealising ex-partners
76	Anxious/Avoidant trap
80	Accountability - have you been a lone wolf?
83	*If you are ... the avoidant partner*
84	Emotional bank
85	When your partner speaks up
86	Ups & Dows
87	*If you are <u>with</u> the avoidant partner*
88	Jingsaw analogy
89	Are you abandoning yourself?
90	Your gift
91	Thank you!

PROLOGUE

I am a business owner living in a small town in Europe. I've faced my share of relationship challenges over the years, bumping into hurtful situations along the way. Today, I'm thrilled to share that I'm in a happy and secure marriage. This workbook serves as encouragement for you to persist in your search for solutions, and never give up. You deserve to experience a loving relationship, one that brings out the best in both you and your partner.

Understanding my attachment style has been incredibly helpful. It has allowed me to:

1. Recognise and understand why healthy relationships often feel challenging, while toxic or unhealthy relationships feel easier to fall into.
2. Reduce anxiety and uncertainty in my interactions, no longer having to wonder, "What did I do wrong?"
3. Learning how to become a better parent, friend, and companion by being more aware of my attachment style.

When I first embarked on this journey, seeing my attachment patterns clearly was quite overwhelming. In particular, when it came to my avoidant attachment style, I often felt lost and misunderstood. The world is not very friendly to avoidants. We are often misunderstood, blamed, and sometimes discarded.

It wasn't until I heard a social worker speak about avoidant attachment with understanding and compassion that my whole world changed. For the first time in my life, I felt truly understood and supported.

Through this workbook, my goal is to share with you the same sense of relief and hope I felt that day. Within these pages, you'll discover a list of helpful exercises that will provide guidance and support on your journey as a dismissive-avoidant.

Are you really afraid of commitment?

As someone with a dismissive avoidant attachment style, you have probably been told all your life that you are afraid of commitment. To begin this workbook, we'll kick things off by challenging this belief.

Write a comprehensive list of every commitment you have right now, or have had in the recent past. These can be in the context of your workplace, home life, or community (for instance, that promise you made your neighbour to look after their dog).

Once your list is finished, answer the following questions for every single commitment you noted down.

LIST OF COMMITMENTS

On a scale from 1 to 10, how important do you feel these commitments are? How much of a burden do they have on your life? (1 being the lowest and 10 being the highest)

How important do you feel these commitments are?

1   2   3   4   5   6   7   8   9   10

How much of a burden do they have on your life?

1   2   3   4   5   6   7   8   9   10

How important do you feel these commitments are?

1   2   3   4   5   6   7   8   9   10

How much of a burden do they have on your life?

1   2   3   4   5   6   7   8   9   10

How important do you feel these commitments are?

1   2   3   4   5   6   7   8   9   10

How much of a burden do they have on your life?

1   2   3   4   5   6   7   8   9   10

How important do you feel these commitments are?

1 2 3 4 5 6 7 8 9 10

How much of a burden do they have on your life?

1 2 3 4 5 6 7 8 9 10

How important do you feel these commitments are?

1 2 3 4 5 6 7 8 9 10

How much of a burden do they have on your life?

1 2 3 4 5 6 7 8 9 10

How important do you feel these commitments are?

1 2 3 4 5 6 7 8 9 10

How much of a burden do they have on your life?

1 2 3 4 5 6 7 8 9 10

How important do you feel these commitments are?

1 2 3 4 5 6 7 8 9 10

How much of a burden do they have on your life?

1 2 3 4 5 6 7 8 9 10

Identifying and understanding your current commitments may not lead to a significant breakthrough, but can help shine a light on the fact that you are more comfortable with commitments than you think you are. You are able to follow through with responsibilities, with friends, at work, and even with strangers. Maybe having an avoidant attachment style is more nuanced than others decide to reduce it to.

How do your role models deal with commitments?

Me		My role models
	Work	
	Health	
	Family	
	Friends	
	Romantic relationships	
	Education	
	Self improvement	
	Fun and recreation	
	Finances	

Are you really afraid of dependency?

You've likely also heard that you have a fear of losing your independence. But is it really dependence you are afraid of, or do you resist being manipulated into doing something?

If you have experienced parentification or enmeshment, you might have stepped into the role of the "lost child". This concept describes a role within a family, where the child is often used as a pawn in family conflicts. They are usually overlooked, putting their needs aside as the family dynamics take precedence. Your apprehension isn't about depending on or being depended upon; rather, you simply want to engage in experiences without hidden agendas.

Why you will benefit from a workbook for Avoidant attachment

When I first started on my journey, I quickly encountered a barrier. I soon realised that I had a fearful-avoidant attachment style, which is a combination of both avoidant and anxious tendencies. As soon as I started looking into all the resources available online, I discovered that there weren't many self-help books tailored specifically for avoidants, and this slowed my progress.

Most books and videos describing attachment styles were not equipped enough to effectively support avoidants. Furthermore, even psychologists frequently gloss over the issue, often offering advice such as "Share your emotions freely, speak up more, and don't be dismissive!"

It wasn't until I had a conversation with a social worker that I finally understood how to support my attachment style. Since that pivotal moment, my journey has been fulfilling. I've gathered various exercises and resources that have helped me cultivate and achieve a secure attachment with my longtime partner.

Certain exercises may initially feel counterintuitive, while others may provide fresh perspectives. I hope they will be as beneficial to you as they were to me many years ago when I used them to establish a beautiful and stable relationship.

What is attachment?

Our childhood experiences and interactions with those who are close to us significantly influence our future relationships with others. This phenomenon is commonly referred to as "attachment".

The way we form attachments to others is primarily shaped by our interactions with our mother or other primary caregiver, and how they relate to us. It mostly depends on how they respond to our needs. Our attachment style generally begins to develop in the first 18 months of our lives, making this the most crucial period for our future relationships.

This significance is rooted in the fact that humans are born extremely underdeveloped compared to other mammals. While some animals can learn to walk within a few hours of birth, we, as infants, struggle to lift our heads for several weeks. Our survival hinges on receiving assistance for every aspect of our well-being, making it crucial for our caregivers to respond to our needs adequately.

During this 18-month period, our brains undergo constant and rapid development. We continually gain a deeper understanding of the world around us, and we internalise the stimuli we receive from our caregivers. Essentially, we learn from them what care and love entail, and this knowledge becomes ingrained in our psyche, influencing our behaviours and attitudes in our later lives.

If our caregivers fail to provide adequate responses to our needs during this formative period, we may inadvertently adopt these behaviour patterns that will shape our future attachments.

Attachment in psychology

The first observations on attachment in the 1950s primarily focused on children, but subsequently, researchers identified adult attachment patterns as well.

Type A: Dismissive-Avoidant.

As children, individuals with this attachment style tend to be more exploratory, giving less attention to their caregiver. They often shy away from their parent's approach, frequently experiencing insecurity and restlessness in close proximity.

Typically, their caregivers exhibit less sensitivity to the child's needs, often providing inadequate responses or none at all. Consequently, these children learn to self-soothe and become self-reliant, as they acquire that there is no accessible support during times of need.

The adult counterpart of this avoidant type is known as Dismissive-Avoidant. These adults have difficulties in forming relationships, and even if they do manage to do so, they may prematurely end the relationship or actively engage in behaviours that lead to its end.

The most prominent factors contributing to these behaviours include a reluctance to lose their independence. They have a hard time expressing their emotions and also struggle to deal with other people's emotions. This challenge primarily stems from a lack of early learning in emotional regulation, as their caregiver didn't respond appropriately to their emotional needs.

As a result, these individuals yearn for attention, love, and empathy, but when their needs are met, they often feel overwhelmed. This can occur because they either don't believe they deserve such care or they fear the vulnerability that comes with opening up emotionally, which may come with emotional manipulation from others. Trusting others is a significant challenge for them, as they often see themselves as "okay" but perceive their partners as "manipulative - not okay".

Attachment style	You	Partner
Secure	Okay	Okay
Avoidant	Okay	Not okay
Anxious	Not okay	Okay
Disorganized	Not okay	Not okay

Type B: Secure.

Caregivers of children with this second attachment style tend to answer their child's needs in a consistently adequate manner. They mirror back their emotions, calming them when they are upset or in distress, and are generally available during times of need. These children balance their time between exploration and seeking closeness with their caregivers equally.

The adult version of the secure attachment type is also referred to as "Secure". These individuals easily form new relationships and find it relatively straightforward to enjoy them. They are comfortable with emotional openness in their relationships and are receptive to their partner's feelings.

They do not fear losing their independence as a result of their bonds, and find it easier to fully commit to their relationships. They perceive both themselves and their partner as being "okay".

Type C: Anxious-Ambivalent.

This third attachment style is characterised by caregivers who tend to be inconsistent and unreliable in their responses. They may provide conflicting answers to the same calls for help from their children, such as calming them when they cry on one occasion and neglecting or even mocking them on the next.

As a result, these children don't actively seek closeness with their caregivers, nor do they engage in much exploration. They remain constantly vigilant and alert because they are uncertain about what to expect.

The adult pair of this type is called Anxious-Preoccupied. These adults excessively search for validation and approval from others, constantly searching for opportunities to form relationships. While they might readily enter and settle into partnerships, their emotional expression tends to be rather ambivalent.

They oscillate between suppressing their emotions and overwhelming their partners with them. They constantly monitor their environment, searching for signs of approval or disapproval. They are prone to idolising their partner while feeling dissatisfied with themselves. Typically, they see themselves as "not okay" and their partner as "okay".

Type D: Disorganised.

This fourth and final attachment style was added by experts much later to accommodate those who didn't fit into the first three styles. It is even debated whether the disorganised type constitutes a distinct attachment style, or rather represents the lack of one.

Parents of individuals with this style often exhibit patterns of emotional, physical, or even sexual abuse, as well as neglect. In some cases, these parents may use the children as emotional punching bags. Children in this group respond negatively to both the absence and the presence of their caregivers.

Type D's adult counterpart is Fearful-Avoidant. They long for intimacy but also fear it, as they are hesitant to trust others. They are concerned about potential disappointments and emotional wounds, and their feelings about intimacy are complex. They see both themselves and their partners in a negative light, oscillating between feeling unworthy of their partner and being mistrustful of them. They have difficulty expressing their emotions and often suppress them as a result. They tend to see both themselves and their partners as "not okay".

You might have noticed that all the attachment styles, except for the secure one, use different names for children and adults. While there are many similarities between the attributes and attitudes of the age groups, the naming convention is based on the most perceptible traits.

Children vs adults

Avoidant children are, most notably, insecure. They struggle to establish a genuine connection with their caregivers. They are aware of their difficulty in trusting others and often find it challenging to find their role and place in the world.

In the case of avoidant adults, meanwhile, though their insecurities persist, they tend to downplay the significance of relationships. They often think that they are better off alone.

The Anxious attachment style follows the same pattern. Children are ambivalent, driven by anxiety that stems from their inability to predict how the caregiver will react to their needs or actions. In contrast, adults tend to become preoccupied, as they proactively seek ways to ensure they please their partner in any way they believe will be most satisfying to them.

Children with a Disorganised attachment style struggle to establish consistent and stable connections. After a hint of kindness from someone they will eagerly seek affection, but their demeanor can quickly shift when faced with simple requests, like cleaning their room.

Fearful-Avoidant adults, on the other hand, might exhibit a more sophisticated outward display of emotion, but their possible traumas still make them avoid relationships. Unlike the avoidance and dependency issues seen in Type A attachment, their reluctance is driven by the fear caused by their emotional traumas.

Note that, while most people fall into one attachment category, identifying some traits in yourself doesn't necessarily mean that you squarely fit into that particular one. While our primary attachment type mostly consolidates by around 18 months of age, ongoing experiences and personal growth can continue to shape our attitudes toward relationships and intimacy.

QUIZ

Please consider how true the following statements are for you in your relationships and rate them on a scale from 0 to 3. There are no right or wrong answers, so be honest as much as possible.

1. I can respect the needs and boundaries of my partner.

    0   Not true at all

    1   Generally not true

    2   Generally true

    3   Completely true

2. I can deeply engage in a relationship.

    0   Not true at all

    1   Generally not true

    2   Generally true

    3   Completely true

3. I have a hard time coping with loneliness.

    0   Not true at all

    1   Generally not true

    2   Generally true

    3   Completely true

4. The thought of committing to someone scares me.

- 0   Not true at all
- 1   Generally not true
- 2   Generally true
- 3   Completely true

5. When I'm in a relationship, I want to be alone, but when I'm alone, I long for a relationship.

- 0   Not true at all
- 1   Generally not true
- 2   Generally true
- 3   Completely true

6. It's not difficult for me to talk about my emotions.

- 0   Not true at all
- 1   Generally not true
- 2   Generally true
- 3   Completely true

7. I feel like I have a hard time connecting with others.

- 0   Not true at all
- 1   Generally not true
- 2   Generally true
- 3   Completely true

8. I generally strive for independence within a relationship.
   - 0   Not true at all
   - 1   Generally not true
   - 2   Generally true
   - 3   Completely true

9. I feel like I have to meet the expectations of my partner(s).
   - 0   Not true at all
   - 1   Generally not true
   - 2   Generally true
   - 3   Completely true

10. I often find it tiring when my partner talks to me about their emotions.
    - 0   Not true at all
    - 1   Generally not true
    - 2   Generally true
    - 3   Completely true

11. I'm afraid of getting disappointed or hurt in a relationship.
    - 0   Not true at all
    - 1   Generally not true
    - 2   Generally true
    - 3   Completely true

12. It's difficult for me to open up to others.
    - 0 Not true at all
    - 1 Generally not true
    - 2 Generally true
    - 3 Completely true

13. I enjoy being in a romantic relationship, but I can also feel comfortable being alone.
    - 0 Not true at all
    - 1 Generally not true
    - 2 Generally true
    - 3 Completely true

14. I often feel like I can't trust others.
    - 0 Not true at all
    - 1 Generally not true
    - 2 Generally true
    - 3 Completely true

15. I feel like I can easily build relationships.
    - 0 Not true at all
    - 1 Generally not true
    - 2 Generally true
    - 3 Completely true

16. I want harmonious relationships, but I feel incapable of forming connections with others.
    - 0   Not true at all
    - 1   Generally not true
    - 2   Generally true
    - 3   Completely true

17. I often feel like I can't keep my emotions to myself.
    - 0   Not true at all
    - 1   Generally not true
    - 2   Generally true
    - 3   Completely true

18. I often fear that I will mess things up in my relationships.
    - 0   Not true at all
    - 1   Generally not true
    - 2   Generally true
    - 3   Completely true

19. I'm afraid that talking about my feelings makes me vulnerable.
    - 0   Not true at all
    - 1   Generally not true
    - 2   Generally true
    - 3   Completely true

20. I feel like I have a hard time committing to my partner(s).
- 0 Not true at all
- 1 Generally not true
- 2 Generally true
- 3 Completely true

21. I'm afraid of being alone.
- 0 Not true at all
- 1 Generally not true
- 2 Generally true
- 3 Completely true

22. I believe I can function well in a romantic relationship.
- 0 Not true at all
- 1 Generally not true
- 2 Generally true
- 3 Completely true

23. I don't know what to expect from my partner.
- 0 Not true at all
- 1 Generally not true
- 2 Generally true
- 3 Completely true

24. I often become suspicious when people show positivity towards me.

- 0   Not true at all
- 1   Generally not true
- 2   Generally true
- 3   Completely true

25. Dating is not a problem, but I find it hard to deepen my relationships.

- 0   Not true at all
- 1   Generally not true
- 2   Generally true
- 3   Completely true

26. I feel like neither I nor my partner(s) can function harmoniously.

- 0   Not true at all
- 1   Generally not true
- 2   Generally true
- 3   Completely true

27. I frequently worry about what my partner thinks of me.

- 0   Not true at all
- 1   Generally not true
- 2   Generally true
- 3   Completely true

28. It's not hard for me to commit to a romantic relationship.
    - 0   Not true at all
    - 1   Generally not true
    - 2   Generally true
    - 3   Completely true

Now add up the scores of the items as stated below:

Avoidant:	7	8	10	12	19	20	25
Secure:	1	2	6	13	15	22	28
Anxious:	3	9	17	18	21	23	27
Disorganised:	4	5	11	14	16	24	26

The attachment style with the biggest score may be the most typical for you. How to add up the values? If your answer to the first question is 2. Then you need to add 2 points to the secure attachment style.

Your score:

Avoidant: _____
Secure: _____
Anxious: _____
Disorganized: _____

To keep in mind, this is in no way a standardised attachment test, only a tool to give you a grasp of the tendency of your attachment style.

Why does Avoidant attachment exist?

In Attached, the most influential book on attachment theory, Levine and Heller describe attachments as evolutionary strategies that developed to increase our survival. For most of our ancestral history, small communities sustained themselves by working together.

However, in case of disease, hunger, and natural disasters, different survival skills became important. These included being independent, self-sufficient, and detached. Being avoidant became a necessity. In a dangerous and unpredictable environment, it might not be advantageous to invest time and energy attaching to one person, as they may not be likely to be around for very long.

As someone who grew up in a chaotic family, where it was not possible to predict or build emotional safety with my caregivers, it was easy to detach myself. I thought that I had to take care of everything on my own, and this belief extended into my adult life. Nature doesn't always trigger what is "best" or what guarantees our utmost happiness. It often guides us towards what is "good enough."

What are the advantages of being Avoidant?

- Personal growth and self-discovery, as you often prioritise your goals and hobbies
- Independence, confidence, and self-reliance
- Adaptability, as you may find it easier to embrace changes in your life since you are not completely dependent on one situation
- The ability to establish and maintain boundaries, inspiring others to set their boundaries as well
- Open-mindedness towards new situations and new groups
- Emotional detachment can be helpful in situations of distress
- Self-soothing and autonomy
- Low-maintenance

Of course, nothing can truly replace the loving presence of a friend, family member, or partner who can really be there for you during challenging times. Through this exercise, I am not trying to minimise the importance of relationships. Instead, I aim to highlight that being avoidant can have positive outcomes. Before the world shames or resents you for taking time and space for yourself, please consider that the following skills have played a vital role in helping you navigate your day-to-day.

Please take a moment and write down some situations where being avoidant has been helpful for you and why.

Write down times when you wish you hadn't been avoidant. Are there occasions when it would have been helpful to have a bit of faith, and open up more?

What is the next step?

According to the book The Courage to Be Disliked, happiness is sustained by two pillars:
- Self-reliance
- Belonging to a community

You have already achieved and mastered self-reliance. You know you can count on yourself! The second pillar of happiness is belonging. I hope that the following workbook will help you develop the skills you need to achieve fulfilling emotional intimacy with your loved ones.

What you might get wrong about healing Avoidant attachment

Many individuals believe that healing insecure attachment means healing the past. It's a logical assumption, as the past shapes our present. As a 'recovered avoidant' myself, I hold a different belief. Healing avoidant attachment is more about healing the future than the past.

What is the main reason for your avoidance? You are predicting you will get hurt.

Even if you are surrounded by love and affection, your interpretation and apprehension of the future are preventing you from embracing connections that may already be there, or have the potential to develop.

How can you stop forecasting a future full of loneliness and pain?

"The secret of life lies within those milliseconds between stimulus and response." Steven Covey

While it may sound simplistic, the solution can often be straightforward. You start predicting a better future by employing two strategies.

Did you know that according to a 2006 Oxford study, avoidants frequently struggle to identify their emotions? By cultivating self-awareness of your inner experience, you can shift from reactivity to "response-ability".

The first step involves recognising when your thoughts are entangled in the past. Remember, your past doesn't need you, but your future does! When you truly achieve awareness, the present connection you share with someone is no longer something you need to escape from, you can fully embrace the potential of the present.

The second phase requires you to start creating new memories. Most individuals have 95% of the same thoughts from the previous day. How can you expect a different life from yesterday if your thoughts remain the same?

You need to teach your brain that what you want exists in order for it to feel safe and familiar.
By fostering secure experiences, you can create new neural pathways, gradually increasing your comfort in secure relationships. The good news is that you can start this process by simply spending more time with friends you like and trust. Even if you can't overwrite negative memories, creating new ones will reinforce pathways that lean toward trust and positivity.

SEARCH FOR GLIMMERS

The word 'glimmer' is usually associated with small, radiant reflections of light. However, in a psychological context, 'glimmers' represent the opposite of triggers. Glimmers are internal or external cues that calm your nervous system because they provide reassurance and hope 🤝

Think of the last time you felt well and **hopeful** in company of one or more people. Write down their names:

Next to their name, write down what particular **feature** or **characteristic** made you feel well and safe next to them. Sometimes we don't know exactly what makes a person **feel safe**, but try writing it down anyways. It can be their **tone of voice, gentle smile, common interests, a particular book** you both like.

SEARCH FOR GLIMMERS

Think of ways you could spend time with the people you described? In the following exercise, write down some future ideas.

Name	Future Ideas

SEARCH FOR GLIMMERS

Glimmers can also be **spaces**. For a long time, I was really into hiking over hills. Not necessarily mountains, it had to be specifically hills. It was such a specific request that everyone around me found it a bit funny. As I was approaching my hike one day, somehow everything came into place and the image of the hill somehow overlapped with an image of **my grandparents' house**, also placed on a hill. That connection reminded me of a **safe place** as they have always been careful and supportive.

Write down locations where you would feel a **sense of safety** (Even if you don't fully understand why).

Think if you could include the following **destinations** into your **future plans**. It can be as simple as visiting the coffee place you really like. You don't have to **stress about making plans yet**, just think and **write down** about the **future possibilities**.

- [ ] _____
- [ ] _____
- [ ] _____
- [ ] _____
- [ ] _____
- [ ] _____
- [ ] _____
- [ ] _____
- [ ] _____

What type of burden are you carrying?

While all attachment styles are complex and can be influenced by various factors, parentified children have higher chances of becoming avoidants. Parentification happens when a child takes on the role of the parent or caregiver in their early years. The extra responsibility is in no way adequate for a young child who is not developmentally prepared for this role. This additional burden can take place under one or more conditions.

Instrumental parentification

In instrumental parentification, a child is assigned the responsibility of carrying out various family chores. This may encompass tasks such as handling household chores, cooking, cleaning, and tending to younger siblings. Essentially, the child assumes the responsibilities of a caregiver or housekeeper.

The children might even be required to make significant life decisions or participate in adult discussions, instead of having the opportunity to focus on their own growth, education, and development.

For immigrant families, this might mean acting as a translator when the caregivers are not fluent in the predominant language. For other children, it could mean providing medication for a parent with disabilities or feeling responsible for a caregiver with addiction.

While there can be periods of crisis in every family, during which children are required to take on additional responsibilities, this practice is in no way fair for the youngsters, and should not be sustained for a long period of time.

Sibling parentification

Sibling parentification is a situation where an older sibling steps into parental roles for their younger brothers and sisters. This often takes the form of fulfilling tasks such as feeding, bathing, changing diapers, and providing emotional support.

In certain cases, the siblings might act as protectors, generally looking after younger siblings, ensuring their safety, or providing reassurance. While in other situations, they might provide educational guidance, and help younger siblings navigate the general challenges of school.

Unfortunately, being put in this position can potentially lead to feelings of stress, resentment, and a lack of typical childhood or adolescent experiences.

Financial parentification

In the case of financial parentification, a child may be required to make financial contributions to their family. This takes the form of working at a young age to provide additional income, supporting household budgeting decisions, or even taking on the entire family's financial responsibilities. Financial burdens can place emotional and psychological strain on children, as they may begin to experience a sense of helplessness.

Emotional parentification and partner substitution

In emotional parentification, a child is expected to provide emotional support, comfort, and stability to one or both parents. This may involve consoling a distressed or emotionally needy parent, acting as a confidant, or being a source of emotional reassurance.

In this type of parentification, a child may be called upon to fulfil the emotional needs of a parent who lacks suitable adult companionship in the form of a spouse or partner. The child might become the primary source of companionship instead, and the boundaries between parent and child become blurred.

This situation is more commonly associated with avoidant attachment styles and can be referred to as enmeshment or emotional incest, depending on the circumstances.

While we cannot change our past, I encourage you to explore the following exercise. It will help you identify which area is more triggering for you, leading to a better understanding of yourself and improved communication with others.

PARENTIFICATION EXERCISE

Begin this exercise by ticking the boxes where you felt most affected during your childhood. Then, take a moment to identify which category has had the most significant impact on you. This will be the category with the most boxes ticked.

Instrumental parentification

- Helping with chores around the house, like cooking and cleaning.
- Managing the family's money and making sure bills were paid.
- Organising family events and making special moments happen.
- Feeling like your worth was connected to how well you managed things at home.
- Administering or managing family members' medicine.
- Having to make difficult decisions.
- Serving as a translator in families where the parent does not speak the primary language of their resident country.

Sibling Parentification:

Caring for and helping your younger siblings with daily tasks like feeding and bathing.

Keeping an eye on your younger siblings and making sure they were safe.

Offering emotional support, comfort, and guidance to your younger siblings.

Helping your younger siblings with schoolwork and guiding their learning.

Feeling responsible for the well-being and care of your younger siblings.

Having resentment, and a lack of a typical childhood or adolescence.

Financial Parentification

Earning money to help support your family, often by working part-time jobs.

Assisting in managing the family's money and ensuring bills were paid on time.

Putting your family's financial needs above your own.

Handling grown-up money responsibilities like bill payments.

Feeling worried about the family's financial situation and wanting to help.

Emotions Parentification / Partner Substitution

Feeling like only your parents emotional needs matter, not being able to express/have space for your own emotional needs.

Feeling the burden of your parents' emotions.

Being afraid of disappointing your parents as soon as you ask for emotional distance.

Feeling no clear boundaries, often acting more like a parent than a child. Being addressed as an adult and often feeling like a therapist.

Being exposed to adult problems like one caregiver confiding in you about their partner's affairs, and feeling that you are held responsible.

You had to soothe yourself AND your parents.

Conclusions

We all have our triggers. If you hate it when coworkers don't wash their dishes or leave a mess, maybe it's because a lot of these kinds of responsibilities fell on you as a kid? (instrumental parentification)

If you dislike individuals that overspend and never follow a budget, maybe you had to be very financially conscious as a teenager? (financial parentification)

If you hate it when acquaintances emotionally dump on you, maybe you are tired of being everyone's therapist? (emotional parentification)

> Or ... maybe you just don't like individuals that are disrespectful. That's also a valid option. In any case, knowing what triggers you can better help you understand yourself. Additionally, it will allow you to communicate your needs better.

ENMESHMENT

Emotional incest and enmeshment are terms used to describe dysfunctional parent-child relationships.

Emotional incest refers to a dynamic in which a parent turns to their child for emotional support and validation, treating the child more like a partner than a child. The parent may confide in the child about adult issues, share inappropriate emotional burdens, or seek comfort in ways that go beyond the typical parent-child relationship boundaries. This creates a situation where the child is forced to take on the role of the emotional caretaker, abandoning their own needs and boundaries.

Enmeshment, on the other hand, is a family dynamic characterised by blurred emotional boundaries and an excessive level of involvement between family members. In an enmeshed relationship, individual identities become intertwined, making it challenging for a person to develop a sense of self independent of the family unit. There is a lack of privacy, autonomy, and personal boundaries, with family members overly involved in each other's thoughts, feelings, and decisions.

In both cases, children abandon their own sense of self in order to please their caregiver in order to be worthy of love. Which leaves the child feeling emotionally abandoned. In adulthood, avoidants are at peace mostly when they are alone because that was the most positive childhood experience: a situation with no hidden agendas and no emotional manipulative actions to protect from.

Enmeshment in relationships can be a complex and subtle issue, and it may not always be easy to identify. This quiz is designed to help you reflect on your relationships and determine if you may be experiencing enmeshment.

Instructions: For each question, choose the response that best describes your feelings or experiences in your current or past relationships.

Have you ever felt pressured to hide your true feelings, thoughts, or desires to avoid upsetting or disappointing someone close to you?

    a)   Yes, I often hide my true self

    b)   Occasionally, but it depends on the situation

    c)   No, I can express my true self

Have you ever felt guilty when making decisions that may conflict with the wishes or expectations of someone close to you?

- a) Yes, often
- b) Occasionally
- c) Rarely or never

Do you find it difficult to set and maintain personal boundaries in your relationships, often allowing others to invade your personal space, emotions, or time?

- a) Yes, this is a recurring issue
- b) Sometimes, but I'm working on it
- c) No, I can establish healthy boundaries

Do you often feel responsible for another person's emotions, well-being, or happiness?

- a) Frequently
- b) Occasionally
- c) Rarely

Is it challenging for you to distinguish your own needs, desires, and goals from those of your close relationships, such as family members or a partner?

    a)   Yes, I struggle with this

    b)   Sometimes

    c)   No, I can differentiate my needs from theirs

Do you often prioritise the needs and wants of your close relationships over your own, even if it means sacrificing your own happiness or well-being?

    a)   Yes, I do this frequently

    b)   Sometimes, but not always

    c)   No, I prioritise my own needs as well

Have you ever felt trapped or overly dependent on someone in your life, to the point where you feel like you cannot function independently?

    a)   Yes, I have experienced this

    b)   Occasionally, but it's not a constant feeling

    c)   No, I can function independently

Do you struggle to have a clear sense of your own identity, separate from your relationships or the people close to you?

- a) Yes, I find it challenging to define my identity
- b) Sometimes, I'm not sure
- c) No, I have a strong sense of my own identity

Did a parent or caregiver make you their primary source of emotional support, often ignoring or neglecting your emotional needs in the process?

- a) Yes, this was a common pattern
- b) Occasionally, it happened sometimes
- c) No, they generally attended to my emotional needs

Were you exposed to inappropriate conversations or information by a parent or caregiver that made you uncomfortable or violated your boundaries, such as discussions about their romantic relationships, sexual experiences, or personal problems?

- a) Yes, I often encountered such conversations
- b) Occasionally, it happened from time to time
- c) No, this was not a common occurrence

Scoring:

- Give yourself 3 points for every "a" response.
- Give yourself 2 points for every "b" response.
- Give yourself 1 point for every "c" response.

Interpretation:

- **24-16 points:** You may be experiencing a significant level of enmeshment in your relationships and should consider seeking professional help or counselling to address these issues.

- **15-8 points:** You might have occasional tendencies toward enmeshment, but it may not be a pervasive problem. Still, it's essential to be aware of these tendencies and work on establishing healthy boundaries.

- **1-8 points:** Your responses suggest that you have a relatively healthy level of autonomy and boundaries in your relationships. However, it's always valuable to keep improving and maintaining healthy boundaries to ensure your well-being.

What are you really feeling?

In your life as an avoidant, you've probably heard many times that you should simply be more open. How can you achieve that when you're not even sure about your own emotions?

As the saying goes, "Men would rather climb a mountain than talk about emotions." To anyone who may have been criticised or judged for not opening up enough, there is one important point to make. Going for a walk when you're emotionally unsettled can be helpful in clearing your mind. In fact, the bilateral stimulation occurring in the brain is one component of EMDR, a successful practice that aids in processing emotional distress more rapidly in your life.

This leads to the point that the strategies you're currently employing - engaging in activities such as sports, work, or other hobbies - are not entirely off. They can provide relief in processing your subconscious emotions and events.

What you're doing in the short term has its merits. However, it might not be the most effective long-term approach for dealing with emotional distress, as those feelings can come up time and again.

So, why should you shift your focus toward emotions when your short-term strategy seems to be working? To clarify, it's not something you should do for others; Rather, it's a process of self-integration and self-understanding because you spend most of your life flying under the radar. That, in itself, is a pity.

As avoidants, we often suppress our needs, especially if we grew up in emotionally cold or neglectful families. Moreover, we have become adept at dismissing our emotions, which are often great indicators and reminders of those very needs.

While the previous chapter focused on predicting a brighter future with others, this chapter centres on envisioning a better future with yourself.

First, you will learn to identify your emotions. Then, you will acquire the necessary skills to deal with these emotions. Once you grasp the techniques involved, it will all be easier. Suddenly emotions won't feel like a burden.

Learning to manage your emotions will lead to a better understanding of how to deal with them. For us avoidants, especially raised in emotionally neglectful families, it's not that common. I imagine that you (much like myself) often find it hard to identify your own emotions. Of course, you could choose to dismiss them, remove yourself from the situation, or seek distraction elsewhere. However, in doing so, you will be at the whim of circumstances, swept away by feelings you are unsure of. Unless ... you see emotions for what they truly are: a natural feedback mechanism.

The Burning Stove

When you accidentally put your hand on a burning stove, your immediate reaction will be to remove that hand as soon as possible. You might even let out a small scream, or jump up and down right afterward. These are completely normal reactions. This same instinctive response mechanism might happen psychologically, when you experience emotional distress, such as "touching" on a sensitive topic.

In the physical scenario, the first thing that happens is a rapid nerve impulse that travels from your hand to your brain. This impulse carries a clear and urgent message: "This is hot, and it's hurting me. Remove your hand immediately!"

Simultaneously, your body physically responds to the message. Your muscles contract, causing you to quickly withdraw your hand from the hot stove. This tangible response is an automatic, immediate, and often involuntary reaction to protect your well-being.

In this scenario, you might also release a scream or cry. The vocalisation serves as a signal to others in your vicinity that something is wrong, and you need assistance. It's a way of communicating your distress and seeking help.

Now, the key idea behind the 'burning stove' theory is that emotions work in a similar way. When you encounter situations, conversations, or experiences that are emotionally distressing, your emotions serve as a feedback mechanism.

Emotional Signal: Just like the nerve impulse in the physical example above, your emotions send signals to your brain. They convey important information about your experience, such as your feelings of sadness, anger, fear, or discomfort.

Behavioural Response: These emotional signals prompt behavioural responses. For instance, if a conversation is causing you emotional pain, your instinct might be to disengage from that situation. It's a way of protecting yourself from further emotional harm.

Communication: Much like the scream in the physical pain scenario, your emotional expressions (e.g., tears, frustration, or withdrawal) can communicate to others that something is wrong and that you may need support or empathy.

This theory is a metaphor that illustrates how our emotions function to protect us. They alert our brains of potential threats or gains of the material world.

WHY DO EMOTIONS CONFUSE US?

What would happen in a 'burning stove' situation if a caregiver asked their child to stop crying, rather than supporting them in removing their hand from the source of pain? It would certainly sound cruel and hurtful.

Unfortunately, overwhelmed parents are often not aware of the cause of their children's distress- perhaps as a result of their own stress- and therefore condition their children to stop expressing their instinctual emotions instead of finding an appropriate solution.

Over time, the lack of validation could make any child believe that they are not in a safe enough space to express their emotions, or that expressing those emotions causes discomfort to others.
If you lived your life seeing emotions as uncontrollable responses, rather than information, it can be challenging observing them.

As mentioned in the first chapters, let's predict a different future. Even if your caregiver is not present in your day-to-day life anymore, your internalized belief that emotions don't matter may still abound.

HOW TO SAFELY EXPERIENCE EMOTIONS

Have you ever noticed that some of the happiest people tend to be highly connected to and very present in their bodies? When you are in tune with your body, the past and future lose their grip on your thoughts, and your awareness firmly grounds you in the present moment. On the other hand, when you try to escape your own emotions, you might find yourself trapped in a kind of limbo, suspended between the future and the past.

While most experts would suggest you simply acknowledge and feel your current emotions, there's more to it than that. However, there is something incomplete about it. By doing so, you are essentially opening and examining the emotional wound within you. However, it's equally important to learn how to "close" that wound.

The reason individuals like me, and many other avoidants, dismiss our own feelings is because they are simply too painful, distant, and unfamiliar. In fact, "opening the wound" can make us feel even more exposed and vulnerable.

With the following exercise, you will be able to safely explore your emotions, while also taking steps to "close the wound".

The technique is known as R.A.I.N., a method popularised by Tara Brach to effectively manage and navigate difficult emotions and challenging situations. I advise you listen to her online meditation for better results.

R.A.I.N.

**Find a quiet place, where you feel comfortable.
Start by doing a mental scan, sensing if something is pressing in your body**

◆ Is a part of you asking for healing and attention?

◆ Is there something lingering that you are having a hard time with?

◆ Do you feel you have been judging yourself today?

◆ Are you anticipating something negative is going to happen?

With bravery, bring any of those identified feelings closer to you, just so you can sense them fully. You don't have to do anything more, just understand that there is an emotion inside of you that needs to be addressed and cared for.

R of RAIN = Realise and name whatever emotion you're experiencing right now.

_____
_____
_____
_____
_____
_____
_____
_____

<pre>
        ↑
        |
   R   A   I   N
   ─   ─
        |
        ↓
</pre>

A of RAIN = Allow.
Let it be there. You don't have to do anything, you don't have to fix anything.
It's ok, let it belong. It takes maturity and courage to just pause with that feeling, and just let it be.

I of RAIN = Investigate.

> What is this feeling trying to tell you?

You might sense what you're believing, what's going to go wrong, what's wrong with you... and then direct your focus to where that feeling resides in your body.

It takes courage to connect directly with that aspect of yourself, as it is a vulnerable space that you're intentionally addressing at this moment.

> Where are you feeling this sensation in your body?

R A I N

You might sense the most vulnerable part of this experience and where that vulnerability is strongest and then asking: *"What does this place need? What's the flavor of nurturing it most needs?"*

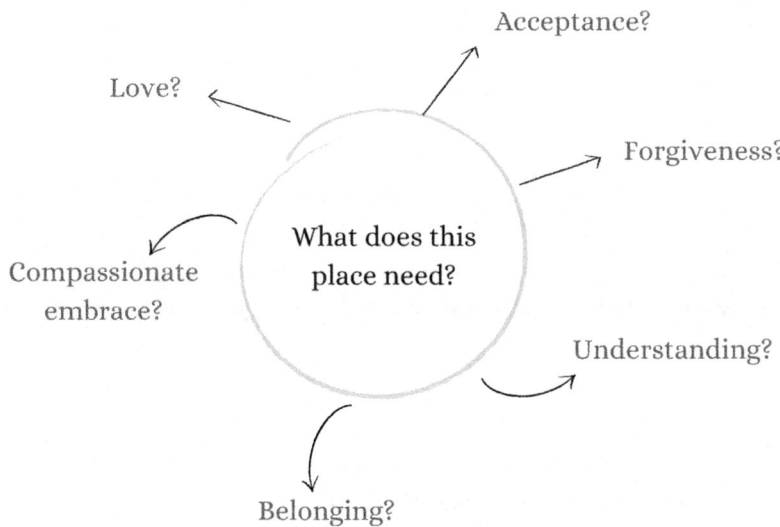

As you focus your attention, connect with the witness within you, that most compassionate aspect of your being. Consider how you can offer kindness to this place of vulnerability right now. Allow your touch to be authentically gentle, conveying care and sending a message to this inner space, reassuring yourself that you can have full confidence in your own inherent goodness and your sense of deserving love. That truly it's okay.

R A I N

N of RAIN = Nurturing.

Can you let in the nurturing? Sometimes the most challenging of all is to let love, light, warmth. This message can come from grandmother, friend, teacher, therapist, someone you trust.

Take a few moments to perceive the transition, whether it's subtle or substantial, from your anxious self to a state of compassion.

Take a few moments to perceive the transition, whether it's subtle or substantial, from your anxious self to a state of compassion. Recognise that this sense of openness and loving presence represents a truer reflection of your essence than any self-narrative. Allow this realisation to strengthen your trust in your fundamental goodness.

The final part is the most important, as you are giving yourself the type of care you need, and you are closing the wound.

Feel free to come back to this exercise whenever you are facing a challenging feeling that you want to explore and nurture. By following this exercise, you will be able to acknowledge, understand, validate, and provide yourself with what you require.

Why should you try?

The Phra Phuttha Maha Suwana Patimakon

The Phra Phuttha Maha Suwana Patimakon, also known as the Golden Buddha, is a statue made entirely from gold. What makes it particularly interesting is not only its beauty but also the fascinating story of its discovery.

During a time of conflict and war in Thailand, as a precaution to safeguard the monument from invading Burmese forces and potential theft, the statue was concealed beneath a layer of stucco. The statue remained hidden like this for centuries.

In the mid-20th century, as the Golden Buddha was being relocated to a new temple, cracks began to appear, hinting at something hidden underneath. It was during this process that people made the astonishing discovery that what they originally thought was a simple plaster statue was, in fact, a priceless golden Buddha.

Much like the story of Pandora's Box, where opening it led to numerous troubles, at the end of the box, hope was always present.

therapist: you need to open up more

me: i can't

therapist: why not?

me: let me visualise it for you

🗨 ↻ ♡ ✉

👤 ↻ **curlicuecal**

It's a good metaphor tho, because the situation is never going to get better if you don't eventually pull the door. And afterwards, no matter what the damage was, you will have a working cabinet, whatever plates you could salvage, and a place to start putting new plates.

CHECK-IN

The following exercise gives you the opportunity to explore and acknowledge your emotions. You don't have to engage with them, just start acknowledging them. You will gain some insights into your inner world.

Start regular self-check-ins by following these steps.

1. Set a few alarms on your phone to remind you to pause and check in with your emotions.

2. When the alarm sounds, take a few deep breaths.

3. Identify and label the emotions you are experiencing without trying to change or suppress them.

Reflective Questions:

1. How did the regular emotional check-ins impact your awareness of your emotions?

2. Did you notice any specific patterns in your emotional experiences throughout the day?

3. How can you use this practice to better understand and regulate your emotions in various situations?

EMOTIONAL SUPRESSION

Avoidants generally try to suppress their emotions. This is the reason why you might back out from a relationship that gets too emotional. Now let's take a look at your own emotional toolkit.

Read through the following list of emotions

Joy	Amusement
Sadness	Boredom
Anger	Loneliness
Fear	Pride
Surprise	Confusion
Disgust	Awe
Excitement	Irritation
Contentment	Nostalgia
Anxiety	Envy
Guilt	Frustration
Jealousy	Anticipation
Hope	Regret
Shame	

EMOTIONAL SUPRESSION

Exercises

◆ Pick 5 emotions that are the easiest for you to experience and really dwell into?

_____
_____
_____

◆ Collect 5 emotions that are the hardest?

_____
_____
_____

◆ In which sense are they difficult? What makes them demanding?

_____
_____
_____
_____

Emotions - the real work

As someone who has suppressed their emotions for a very long time, I can understand why the following chapters may evoke some discomfort.

You would rather jump to the results and actions, while bypassing the fear and shame still present under the hood. For example, wishing to be in a secure relationship already, surrounded by a loving partner and great friends ... but now ask yourself: does this version of yourself feel a lot of shame and fear, or does it offer space and acceptance for these emotions within?

Paradoxically, by suppressing difficult emotions, you are stepping further away from the person you want to become. Remember that emotions serve as a feedback mechanism, and you can always explore them through the R.A.I.N method. There is no need to push them aside any longer.

EMOTIONAL VOCABULARY

Let's start with a challenging emotional state: depression.

Do you currently sense any distress or discomfort within your body? If not, can you recall a past instance when you felt this way? Where did you feel this discomfort in your body?

1 Imagine you are outside a room, take all the distress and push it inside. What do you see? Is it a person, an inanimate object, or a floating sensation?

2 What is this person's/object's job? Is it trying to protect you? Is it trying to give you a burst of energy? Is it trying to break something?

3 Was there a time in your life when this action was absolutely necessary?

4 Now, ask this entity to take a step outside of the room. What lies beyond? Is it your most vulnerable self? What does it need right now? What is something you can give to yourself right now? What would nurture your soul now?

Below you will find a list of emotions. Whenever you experience them, return to this chapter and explore them further.

- **Depression**: What is it protecting you from?

- **Sadness**: What must be released? What do you need to let go of, so that you can make space for something new?

- **Anger**: Which boundaries have been crossed? What needs to be protected and restored?

- **Envy**: What resources do I aspire and wish for, both for myself and others?

- **Fear**: Where do I need to redirect my instincts and energy?

- **Anxiety**: Why do I experience this surge of energy, and what is its purpose?

- **Guilt**: Which values have been disregarded? What must be made right?

Remember, there can be additional clues for emotions:

- If you hold the belief that you are not good enough, it could indicate repressed shame.

- If you have the belief you are not safe, you might have repressed fear.

- Feeling unlovable may be a sign of repressed sadness and grief.

Why should you identify the location of emotion in your body?

I have to admit, one of the reasons why I disliked practising meditation was because I had to pinpoint where the emotion that I was feeling was present in my body. It was too 'New Age' for me. Plus, a part of me was hesitant to fully embrace the experience. However, I came across a metaphor that completely changed my point of view.

It can be explained as follows: Imagine there is a specific ingredient you shouldn't consume, such as lactose. Of course, when you see a milk carton, it's easy to recognize and avoid drinking it. But lactose can often be hidden in different dishes like cakes, lasagnas, and casseroles. Moreover, in today's world, there are many types of milk cartons that look the same but contain almond or rice milk.

In general, it's easy to recognize emotions in their purest form. Anger, for example, is simply anger. But what happens when you experience a mix of emotions?

Much like a recipe where you can't quite pinpoint all the ingredients, emotions often come up in different sizes and flavours. That's why understanding where in your body these emotions manifest can provide valuable insights into identifying them.

Additionally some emotional 'flavours' can be so intense, they often overshadow others. The next time you feel anger, stop for a second and consider: What lies beneath this emotion? Could it be sadness, a sense of disrespect, annoyance, or perhaps a deep feeling of hurt? Anger often emerges when someone or something crosses your inner boundaries. However, it's important to remember that anger is just the surface, with many underlying layers.

By understanding where the emotion manifests in your body, you will better identify and express it both to yourself and to others.

Are you really putting yourself first?

Avoidants have a reputation of being highly independent and self-reliant. It seems like they do whatever they want, always putting themselves first. But is it really the case?

When you spend a lifetime putting up walls, you may find that you don't necessarily have the energy and time to pursue what truly fulfils you. That's why, even when you find someone with whom you can let your guard down, and you can finally pursue your goals, you might feel resentment.

This newfound presence in your life brings with it new needs and desires. Even if your partner is very supportive and encouraging, there is a part of you that feels you are not worthy or lovable, and so you cannot assert your needs in the relationships.

◆ What "emotional walls" are you keeping up?

 What is taking up a lot of energy in your life?

Owning your own wishes

This reminds me of the story in one of Steven's Covey books. During his son's birthday party, he recounted how his son initially hoarded all his birthday presents, not allowing other children to play with them. Only after he had spent enough time playing with them, was he willing to share them with others.

The idea behind this anecdote is that once children get the opportunity to experience something as truly their own, they can begin to learn how to share with others. This is a crucial step in their social and emotional development.

For avoidants, allocating energy to yourself is a significant step. It allows you to eventually find joy in sharing your life with others. Maintaining emotional walls only prevents you from truly using your energy on yourself.

The energy you use to run away from yourself is the same energy you can use to pursue your ideal life. It's one and the same.

When your inner critic surfaces, remember that its role isn't to support you but rather to keep alive the story you have been telling to yourself. If the facade you are trying to keep up is: " I am not lovable", your inner critic will only remind you of it.

♦ What is something you truly want to do, but don't allow yourself to experience?

_____
_____

♦ Go crazy and write down ideas that are a bit 'outside the box'. Maybe something you wouldn't usually dare to do, but would really like to try.

_____
_____

♦ What would happen if you granted yourself permission to pursue it?

_____
_____

In the 2011 book *The Top Five Regrets of the Dying*, the nurse author that interviewed her patients found that most of them have five similar regrets.

1) "I wish I'd had the courage to live a life true to myself, not the life others expected of me."
2) "I wish I hadn't worked so hard."
3) "I wish I'd had the courage to express my feelings."
4) "I wish I had stayed in touch with my friends."
5) "I wish I had let myself be happier."

♦ So let me ask you again, what would you do if you granted yourself permission to be happy?

_____
_____

SABOTAGING INTIMACY

Do you see yourself in the following situations?

Working till late, sometimes missing important events in your partner's life

Being overly critical or judgmental of your partner's flaws

Using humour to deflect from important topics

Keeping parts of your life secret

Insisting on separate vacations

Avoiding making commitments too far in the future

Dating more people at the same time, for a long period of time

Steering away from meeting your partner's parents

You might subconsciously try to sabotage your current or potential relationship. These are all ways to create some distance between you and danger, because the threat of intimacy can be quite scary. Your subconscious will always try to lead you to safety. I don't think you need to blame yourself or feel shame for trying to keep yourself secure.

With the following exercise, try to simply challenge your instinctive thoughts - nothing more.

How are you creating distance?
Avoiding meeting the parents.

Why?
I am afraid they might judge me, and think I am not good enough.

What is underneath the emotion?
Fear.

What is the likelihood they will not like you?
I don't know.

What would happen if I communicated this thought to my partner?
I don't know, I never tried before. They might be understanding.

What would happen if I started predicting a better future?
I never tried it before, so it's worth giving it a try.

Day 1

◆ How are you creating distance?

◆ Why?

◆ What is the underneath the emotion?

◆ What is the likelihood my fear will manifest?

◆ What would happen if I communicated this thought to my partner?

◆ What would happen if I started predicting a better future?

Day 2

◆ How are you creating distance?

◆ Why?

◆ What is the underneath the emotion?

◆ What is the likelihood my fear will manifest?

◆ What would happen if I communicated this thought to my partner?

◆ What would happen if I started predicting a better future?

Day 3

- How are you creating distance?

- Why?

- What is the underneath the emotion?

- What is the likelihood my fear will manifest?

- What would happen if I communicated this thought to my partner?

- What would happen if I started predicting a better future?

HUMANIZING YOUR CURRENT RELATIONSHIP
(OR POTENTIAL RELATIONSHIP)

Let's acknowledge that avoidants are better equipped to notice negative aspects in potential or current partners. The prospect of getting close to someone can feel so risky that our brains will look for ways to sabotage and scout an exit strategy.

These thoughts can look like these examples:
- "They are not ambitious enough. I need someone that inspires me; it can never work."
- "My partner skipped a workout. That's clearly a sign they don't prioritise their health."
- "They are texting too much."
- "They are texting too little."
- "Sometimes they snore at night!"

It's all too easy to fall into a fantasy where we imagine our partner behaving in an ideal, almost superhuman way. But what drives this craving? To the outside world, parents of avoidant individuals often appear quite well organised and may even seem like perfect parents. While they might provide for their children's physical needs, they often lack emotional presence.

This underlying emotional neglect and abuse happens silently in many families. Children often lack the vocabulary for it. Whenever a child does dare to open up about their neglect, perhaps to an aunt, a teacher, or a family acquaintance, they are often dismissed. Many listeners tend to justify parental behaviour by saying, "Well, your parents are only human, after all." This response can trivialise the experience of silent neglect. It's no wonder that it becomes easy to associate the word "human" not just with flaws but with the potential for abuse and neglect to occur again.

That's why for avoidants, being with someone who is not an ideal partner but just "human" can feel like they are being placed in a dangerous situation.

IDEALISING EX-PARTNERS

Avoidant children frequently displayed mistrust towards their caregiver. During childhood, we could sense that something was wrong, leading us to keep a certain distance from our primary caregiver. This doesn't mean that we didn't crave a genuine connection. Perhaps we genuinely desired closeness with our parents ... but from a distance.

So, how did we attempt to achieve this? By creating a fantasy bond. By maintaining a suitable distance, our brains found it safe to recreate a reality where we could experience love within a secure space. In retrospect, this resembles what often happens when we idealise past relationships.

Without the threat of intimacy, we can relive memories from a safe space emotionally, occasionally embellishing them with layers of imagination. The power of the fantasy bond is undeniable. However, sometimes, just half an hour of conversation with an ex can remind us why we ended the relationship in the first place. It's as if the fantasy veil dissipates, and reality kicks in.

When you spend time fantasising about a memory, you unintentionally hinder the creation of new ones. By following the next exercise, you will discover your true needs in a partner, and therefore be able to allocate more time to fulfilling them.

♦ What is something you fantasise about, regarding your ex? Don't overthink it, let your thoughts flow.

♦ What is something you don't actually like about your ex? Be honest. Try to remember details of their personality and character. There must be a few reasons why you broke it off.

What is something you actually like about your ex?

 How can you give yourself permission to pursue those qualities? If you really like your exes because they are adventurous, what is something you can do now to incorporate more adventure into your life? If they were very caring and attentive, how can you give yourself the same attention?

ANXIOUS /AVOIDANT TRAP

Imagine you are driving a brand-new car through a storm. Despite the less-than-ideal weather conditions, you feel calm and confident because you trust your vehicle in all types of weather.

Now, imagine you are driving an older car with a less reliable brake system, broken windshield wipers, and an unpredictable steering wheel. Even if you're facing the same weather conditions as before, this time the storm will have a different impact on you. Since you cannot fully trust your vehicle, you will drive in a state of stress and hyper-vigilance.

This analogy mirrors the experience of anxious attached personalities in relationships. They are often in a heightened state of vigilance and tension. While they aspire to move forward in their relationships, they constantly fear that something might break due to their lack of solid self-foundations.

In this scenario, avoidants also struggle to trust their own vehicle. In case of a storm, they would stop the car and stay stuck in their precarious position. Even when the weather clears, they might be afraid of ever taking the road again, waiting for "perfect" conditions.

Both attachment styles are dysregulated, as neither can fully rely on "their car". While anxious attached personalities will try to change the "outside" conditions, seeking closeness, avoidants would rather completely stop the car, remaining stuck.

Make a list of the times when you felt stuck in your life.

What is something you wish you would have had at that moment? What would have helped you to unstuck?

Anxious & Avoidant often end up together in relationships. Why? Because we are often not looking for someone to heal our wounds, but instead someone to understand them. In theory, an anxious-avoidant relationship sounds nice. However, both parties may struggle to support each other because both cope with life's difficulties in different ways. Anxious personalities seek closeness when they experience emotional distress, while avoidants hope for distance. In a fight-flight-freeze-fawn situation, anxious people are more likely to fawn and fight. While avoidants are more likely to freeze or flee.

The anxious/avoidant trap ensnares both parties when the anxious person's need for closeness makes the avoidant person withdraw even more. This dynamic creates a cycle wherein the anxious person pursues more, and the avoidant person pulls away.

Breaking free from this cycle involves recognising that both attachment personalities would benefit more from "fixing the car" rather than fixating on changing the external conditions or the people around them. Ideally, everyone would be equipped with a resilient car capable of withstanding all types of weather conditions.

In this case, continuing the cycle is unhealthy. If you find yourself at the beginning of such a relationship, you might get the impression that you are fulfilling each other's needs and fears. Avoidants, who struggle with emotional closeness, may perceive anxious individuals as more courageous, taking the initiative in seeking closeness. Meanwhile, for the anxious individuals, the independence and extra space can be a refreshing change from their fear of emotional engulfment.

The tensions and conflicts that surface during this relationship often trap both individuals in a repetitive cycle when they should be focusing on securing their own vehicles instead. There is a peculiar comfort in this pain. Predicting your pain somehow gives you the illusion of control. A familiar hell is still, well, familiar.

As an avoidant, working on your emotional awareness and creating new, secure experiences will help you create a solid foundation. By solidifying the trust in a relationship, you'll gain the confidence to navigate both the ups and downs of life with the knowledge that you can rely on yourself - and others!

❖ Is there a relationship at the moment that is taking away your energy? If yes, write it down.

❖ Is there a way for you to communicate that you are working on yourself and you need some space?

If their reaction is calm and understanding, they probably have a secure attachment. If the individuals you are contacting are upset about your boundaries, then be aware of this dynamic. Remember that healing avoidant attachment can be achieved much easier when surrounded by secure attachments.

This same theory applies to other situations. For example, someone quitting a smoking habit can find it easier to do so when they are surrounded by non-smokers. It doesn't mean that smokers are bad people, only that they are not ideal during recovery. Remember, before you help others, you need to help yourself. "Put on your own oxygen mask first."

ACCOUNTABILITY
HAVE YOU BEEN A LONE WOLF?

When I first started my business, I was frequently advised against being a 'lone wolf'. The message was clear: I shouldn't act independently or in isolation. As an avoidant, I didn't fully understand why. After all, I value independence and self-reliance.

I became so fixated on the idea of doing everything by myself that I failed to recognise when someone was helping or taking a chance on me. The reciprocal energy that should exist in business relationships was absent, and inadvertently, I ended up as a taker.

My perspective changed when I started to give back to those who had supported me, and along with it, my success increased exponentially. Like the main character in My Name is Earl, I decided to make things right by returning favours. Sometimes, it would be enough to just contact them and say a simple 'thank you' was enough. At other times, it meant assisting individuals with completing a milestone, or providing them with support online.

Reconnecting and thanking the people who have helped me has been a heartwarming experience. Often, a short call led to invitations to visit their families or weekend getaway plans.

However, I suggest refraining from contacting individuals who have exhibited any form of abusive behaviour, whether towards you or others. It might sound controversial, but I would also advise against reconnecting with an ex who has an insecure attachment style. Until you have achieved a secure attachment yourself, it's easy to fall into the anxious/avoidant trap.

Make a list of all the friends that have been there for you, even when you least expected it.

-
-
-
-
-
-
-

Write a list of family members who have been on your side when it mattered.

-
-
-
-
-
-

Now list the name of acquaintances, teachers, or strangers that have helped you in unexpected ways.

-
-
-
-
-
-

Next to their name, write down a list of actions that you could take to return the favour. It can be as simple as saying thank you!

THERAPY

While self-reflection is very important, sometimes it can be easier to talk to an expert. I want to remind you that you are not alone, and can always reach out for help. In my experience, therapy has been a helpful tool, uncovering underlying patterns or behaviours that might not have been evident on the surface. That's why I highly recommend reaching out to a trained therapist.

If you've had a bad experience with therapy in the past, or you don't feel comfortable reaching out yet, try to find support in your day-to-day life. Sometimes help can come in unexpected ways. In my case, it was a social worker that encouraged me to look into myself. Sometimes it can be a gentle neighbour, a relative you don't talk to often. In the book The Warrior Way (based on a true story), it was an old man working at a gas station that listened to and encouraged the main character.

IF YOU ARE ...
THE AVOIDANT PARTNER

For everyone that has ever been to a first aid course, you might be surprised how "small things" can make a big difference. Relationships are very similar.

For example, while waiting for the ambulance, a few of the most effective things you can do are:

- Reassuring the individual: "Help is on the way".
- Offer them emotional support.
- Physical proximity: In recovery position, placing your hand on their ribs. Not only to check they are still breathing, but also for the injured person to feel someone in their physical proximity.

For avoidants sometimes it's difficult to understand the inner world of their partner. What might appear trivial from the outside, might feel like an *emergency* internally.

No one is expecting you to be the "doctor" in this situation. However, certain actions can make a big difference for your relationship. Providing reassurance and emotional support are ways of making your loved one feel they are not going through life alone. Simply being physically present, by someone's side, alleviates pain. If you would help a stranger in an emergency situation, why not help your partner?

How can you help my partner next time they need to reassurance?

Pick a few options and experiment with what works best for your relationship.

> Offer your full attention (no distraction, TV in the background, phone messages, etc)
>
> Regular check-ins
>
> Seek to understand first, talk only when you see your partner has finished opening up
>
> Be reassuring with phrases as "I am here for you", "Tell me what bothers you", "I care about you", "What you feel is important"
>
> Understand your partners triggers
>
> Find out their love language and take one step towards them

Your emotional bank

Dr John Gottman is one of the most influential psychologists in the field when it comes to long lasting relationships. In fact, he has helped numerous couples commit to mutual growth, understanding, and happiness.

In order to reach a fulfilling relationship dynamic, he often suggests that couples create an emotional bank. When you make "emotional deposits" within a relationship, you are strengthening your bond, making it easier to feel supported.

Pick one day during the week, which you commit to making your partner happy. If you don't know where to start, I suggest you take the 5 Love Languages Test for both yourself and your partner.

The 5 love languages will give you an indication of which area is important for your partner. This way you can make them feel good by "targeting" exactly what fulfils them.

Words of Affirmation: receiving compliments, encouragement, appreciation and affection.

Acts of Service: running errands, helping with tasks without being asked, noticing when your partner needs something.

Receiving Gifts: thoughtful gifts, small tokens of love and appreciation. It's not about the monetary value, but the sentiment behind the gift and the effort you put into choosing it.

Quality Time: spending meaningful, uninterrupted time with your partner. This can involve activities such as cooking, watching movies, having deep conversations, or simply being present and attentive.

Physical Touch: hugs, kisses, holding hands, cuddling, or any form of affectionate physical contact.

After finding out your partner's love language (usually there is a primary one and a secondary one), commit to one action a week and build up your emotional bank. It can be that initially your partner might not notice.

Especially if their needs haven't been met for a while. You will first need to piece it through and allow your significant other to trust that you are committed to do your best. The more you show up, the more your relationship will blossom.

 How will I invest in my partner's emotional bank this week? What does your significant other need?

When your partner speaks up

Have you ever been to the doctor, hoping to find the cause of your pain or illness, only to be rushed out by the practitioner? Perhaps the office is full of patients waiting in line, or your doctor is having a bad day and *not really listening* or *focusing on all your symptoms.*

Do you remember how frustrating it can feel to be unheard and have your symptoms minimized? It's possible that your significant other might feel the same way. As avoidants, we are often not in touch with our own emotions. Because of that, it can be difficult to actively engage with our partners.

The good news is that your partner doesn't want you to find a "cure". Your loved one only wants you to have the **full picture**. And often it's not about something you did, but something that might have triggered a past memory. We are all carrying some baggage that comes up at unexpected times.

◆ What are some topics your partner often brings up?

_____
_____
_____

Often, it's easy to hear someone else express a problem, if the problem is not related to something you are struggling with personally.

◆ Are any of the previous topics hitting "too close" to home?

_____
_____
_____

Ups & Downs

If you love fire, passion, and the depth of connection you cannot achieve this without also going through some lows. As avoidants, we often dream of regular, predictable relationships. Once we are finally in it, we feel dull, like something is missing.

The following exercise is for you. It's about understanding what you want from a relationship and what your partner needs.

Stable
and
Predictable

Exciting
and
Intense

Place an X on the bar to indicate where you would like your relationship to be. What do you really desire in a partner?

At the end of the day, if you were initially attracted to an emotional partner, it doesn't make sense to change them into something else. Be honest with yourself and write down what you really desire in a partner.

Are you punishing them for something you initially appreciated about them? Is their emotional quality something you wish you had for yourself?

- How can you add more stability to your relationship?

- How can you add more excitement to your relationship?

IF YOU ARE <u>WITH</u> THE AVOIDANT PARTNER

Imagine a cozy evening at home, you and your partner are on the couch and you just ordered take out. One of the best soups in town. As it arrives at your doorstep, and you heat it up, there is just one thing missing: a spoon.

You look at your partner and casually ask them to bring you two spoons. As they are approaching the table, you see them bringing two forks. Confused, you ask them again, to please bring two spoons. This time they place two knives near your plate. At this point, you start getting a bit impatient. "I need a spoon." They look confused and also a bit annoyed, as neither of you can start eating.

What is the moral of this story? Sometimes, your partner doesn't have the right tools. They will bring "to the table" whatever utensils they have available.

Sure, you could bring your own cutlery, all the time. This might sound easy in the beginning, but do you really want to be the one that always has to give in the relationship?

You could tell your partner to go and buy some cutlery. Which is a difficult task for someone that doesn't fully grasp the concept of a spoon. No matter how many times you explain it, for someone not familiar with the concept it's always going to be an uphill battle.

Are you in this relationship for the "potential"?

Why are you asking this person for "spoons"? Why do you need them <u>specifically</u> from this person?

Jigsaw analogy

Jigsaw has been one of the best comedy shows exploring the deepest aspects of relationships. Written and performed by Daniel Sloss, it became famous for its thought-provoking metaphor on relationships.

Imagine that your life is like a jigsaw puzzle. You're just slowly piecing it together, piece by piece, based on the experiences and lessons that you gone through in life until you get the best picture.

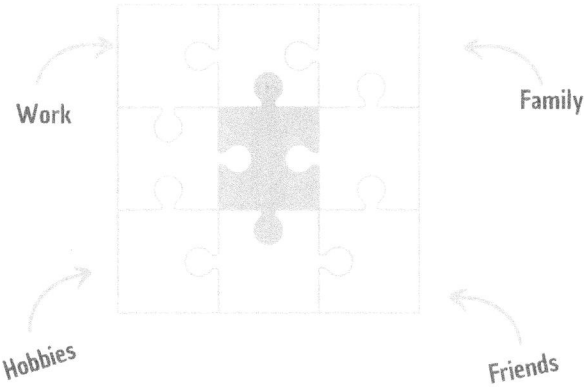

You will start at the four corners: family, friends, hobby/interest, job... And it will vary from person to person. One person might make his family an essential part of their life, another person choose friends or hobbies. However, to complete the jigsaw puzzle, you need its centerpiece, which society often claims to be the perfect partner.

Because we feel under pressure, some of us will make the wrong person the wrong centerpiece and force them into the puzzle, even if they don't really fit.

 Is your partner fitting into your (ideal) life?

Are you abandoning yourself?

- Do you find it easier to do favors to your friend rather than solve something in your life?

- Is it easier to take some extra assignments at work rather than dealing with your own issues?

<u>When you are always ready to help others, you can end up abandoning yourself</u>.

No one denies that getting help from you feels good. At the same time, the people that really care about you, would rather have you focus on yourself, than seeing you sad, disappointed, or maybe even resentful.

What is something you can do for yourself right now?
-
-
-
-
-
-

Every couple is unique, and there is no one-size-fits-all approach to building a fulfilling relationship. However, according to Dr. Gottman, a huge variable that leads to success in a partnership is the *willingness to repair*.

If you have this book in your hands, it means you are willing to work on yourself. This sets you apart from 80% of the population. You are on the right track!

In order to support your growth, I want to offer you the audiobook version for free 🎁 Wishing you the best in your relationship journey!

FREE GIFT

Download your
AUDIO BOOK

Here is your freebie! You can listen to the audio version of this book and reflect on the exercises. To get your free copy, write me at the following email:
alex.kingsman.official@gmail.com

THANK YOU

From all the workbooks you could have picked from, you took a chance and chose this one.

So THANK YOU for readying this workbook and for successfully reaching all the way till the end!

Before you leave, can I ask you a little favor? **Would you take a moment to write a review on the platform?** It's the easiest way to support **independent authors**.

Your insights play a key role in shaping the kind of books I write, ensuring they align with what you're looking for. Your input means a great deal to me, and I'd love hearing from you!

>> Leave a review on Amazon US <<

>> Leave a review on Amazon UK <<

REFERENCES

Levine A., Heller R. (2011). Attached - The New Science of Adult Attachment. Chapter: Dependency is not a bad word. Page 33. Chapter: Decoding relationship behavior. Page 13.

Opie J., McIntosh J. (2019). Early childhood attachment stability and change: a meta-analysis. Attachment and Human Development. Pages 897-930.

Pallini S., Morelli M. Chirumbolo A. (2019). Attachment and attention problems: A meta-analysis. Peer reviewed in Clinical Psychology Review

Rogier G., Muzi S,. Morganti W. ,Pace C (2023). Self-criticism and attachment: A systematic review and meta-analysis - Published on ResearchGate

Walker S. (2022). Emotional intelligence and attachment in adulthood: A meta-analysis - Personality and Individual Differences ScienceDirect

Xiuquin B. (2022). Different effects of anxiety and avoidance dimensions of attachment on interpersonal trust: A multilevel meta-analysis - Research article Sage Journals

Made in the USA
Monee, IL
21 May 2024